THE LI

BI

TIPS

ANDREW LANGLEY

THE LITTLE BOOK OF BREAD TIPS

ANDREW LANGLEY

Absolute Press

First published in Great Britain in 2008 by
Absolute Press
Scarborough House, 29 James Street West
Bath BA1 2BT, England
Phone 44 (0) 1225 316013 **Fax** 44 (0) 1225 445836
E-mail info@absolutepress.co.uk
Web www.absolutepress.co.uk

A catalogue record of this book is available
from the British Library

ISBN 13: 9781904573906

Printed and bound in China by 1010

'If thou tastest a crust of bread, thou tastest all the stars and all the heavens.'

Robert Browning (1812–1889)

1

Put **bread** at the centre of your diet.

It's cheap, nutritious, adaptable and delicious.

There is also something miraculous about the transformation of the hard, chalky dullness of grain into the yielding aromatic scrumptiousness of bread. No wonder the word has been synonymous with food itself for many centuries.

2

Start baking bread today.

Nothing tastes or smells better than bread straight from the oven – except for

your own bread

straight from the oven. The proud sense of achievement never fades, even after decades of home baking.

3

Roll up your sleeves and plunge in.

There's nothing really daunting about breadmaking. It's a remarkably simple process which, once you've mastered the basic technique, takes very little time (twenty minutes of actual work is the rough average).

Just be bold.

4

Try out as many different kinds of bread as possible.

Bread comes in an amazing variety of shapes, textures and tastes. Look out for them in the shops and test them. You'll soon get to know which kinds you like best. Then you can attempt to reproduce them at home.

5

Use a good old-fashioned mixing bowl for your dough.

Ceramic is best, with a white interior, a solid base and an outer rim to grip onto. The bowl should be big enough to hold at least 3$^1/_2$ litres (6 pints) .

6

A big, solid, spacious wooden board is essential

– though a good quality wooden work surface will do as well. A friend in knead, you might say. The bigger the board, the less the mess on the floor.

7

Essential ingredients: flour.

Choose the right kind of flour for what you're baking. For ordinary bread, use a hard, high-protein flour that gives you lots of gluten, which in turn makes the dough elastic. This variety is usually labelled 'Strong Bread Flour'. For griddle cakes and pizzas, use a softer, lower-protein flour.

8

Wholemeal or refined?

Wholemeal flour is just what it says – the whole crushed grain. It makes heavier, denser bread. Flour is refined by sieving out the bran and germ, thus removing the tastiest and most nutritious element. But the resulting bread is lighter.

A judicious mix of the two is best.

9

Stone-ground or metal-rolled?

Conventional mills have steel rollers which squeeze and tear the grain, leaving larger bits to be sieved out.

Stone grinding

crushes the grain more slowly and thoroughly, leaving smaller particles of germ and bran. Some of this escapes the sieve, producing

a better taste

even in refined flour.

10

Essential ingredients: salt.

You only need a little – one scant teaspoon of fine sea salt to 450g (1lb) of flour should do. Salt encourages the gluten proteins to bond happily together, thus producing a nice springy dough.

11

Apart from a mixing bowl and a board, you'll need **a few other simple bits of kit.** For the yeasty mixture, use a medium-sized bowl or jug. Have two wooden spoons to hand for the primary mixing of the flour and liquids, and for scraping out the bowl.

12

Essential ingredients: yeast.

Yeast comes in three forms: fresh (in a moist little block), dried (in granules, to be mixed with water) and instant dried (granules which you add direct to the flour). Fresh is the most exciting to use, and has no added chemicals, but is hard to find in the shops.

13

Remember that yeast is a living organism.

To function properly it needs just the right amount of warm wetness and sugar. Too cold, and the yeast won't get going: too hot, and it will die off. It also needs sugar to convert into the carbon dioxide bubbles which lift the dough.

14

Step 1: making a yeast 'starter'.

Dissolve a teaspoon of sugar, honey or molasses into about 200ml ($^1/_3$ pint) of water at blood heat. Then stir in the yeast (crumbled if it's fresh, sprinkled if it's dried). For each 450g (1lb) of flour, use 25g (1oz) of fresh yeast, or a teaspoon of dried. Leave in a warmish spot.

15

Use a pint glass for measuring out the flour.

Absolute accuracy is not essential, but a pint of flour roughly equals 450g (1lb). To make three loaves, put four pints – 1.8kg (4lbs) – of flour into the mixing bowl. Add salt and mix thoroughly.

16

Essential ingredients: fat.

Fats (or shortening) make bread more tender and light, though they also tend to increase its 'cakeyness'. Use warmed milk, melted butter or lard, or a good cooking oil (sunflower or even olive oil).

17

Step 2: mixing everything together.

Stir 2 or 3 tablespoons of the chosen fat or oil into the yeast starter (which should by now have healthy dobs of foam on top). Make a well in the flour and pour in the mixture. Mix thoroughly with the spoons until the liquid is absorbed.

18

Step 3: adding more tepid water.

The dough will still be very dry and crumbly. Pour in very roughly ½ pint (250ml) more water (The exact amount will vary according to the type of flour you're using). Mix in carefully to avoid slopping and splashing.

19

Experiment with other kinds of wheat flour.

Durum or 'hard' wheat is the most common, but there are some more unusual varieties. Try spelt or kamut, grown by the ancient Egyptians. Both have even higher protein and fibre levels than durum, and add a pleasingly nutty tinge to the bread.

20

How much water?

Stay calm about this. If the dough's too wet (still sticking to the spoon), you can add more flour. If it's too dry, add more water. Simple as that. With a little practice, you will be able to judge instinctively which proportions create the right consistency.

21

Step 4: kneading.

Turn the dough out onto a floured board and begin kneading. Use the heels of your hands to stretch the dough. Then fold it back on itself, squash it and stretch it again. This is a vital process, which encourages the gluten to develop and compresses air into the dough.

22

Take your time with kneading.

It's a contemplative activity that should take – in dull figures – about ten minutes. It gives you the opportunity to become familiar with your dough, fine-tuning the consistency and enjoying the way it comes to life under your hands.

23

Step 5: proving.

Clean the bowl, lightly grease it and put in the dough. Cover with cling film or a cloth and set somewhere draught-free and room temperature for at least 2 hours. Then turn the dough out onto the board again, divide into three.
Shape and put into greased bread tins for another 30 minutes (and no more).

24

You can **speed up** the initial **proving or rising** process by putting the bowl in a warm place. The likeliest spots are inside an airing cupboard, near a radiator or above a warm oven. Best of all, of course, is the top of an Aga.

25

If you're in no hurry, remember:

the slower the rise, the better the taste.

In a moderate or cool temperature, the dough will rise much more slowly. Try leaving it to rise overnight and baking next morning. It will develop a much more interesting flavour and aroma and a chewier texture.

26

Step 6: baking.

When the dough is in the tins, preheat the oven to 230°C (450°F). After 30 minutes, slash the tops gently with a sharp knife and put in the oven. Bake for about 35 minutes, when it's nice and brown but not charring. Remove and turn out to cool on a wire rack.

27

Check that the bread is thoroughly cooked. Turn the loaf over and tap the bottom with a knuckle. If it sounds hollow, it's ready. If it sounds dull, it needs a few more minutes in the oven (there's no need to put it back in the tin though).

28

Store cooled bread in a bin or a freezer.

Wrapping is needed for the freezer, but not the bin. At room temperature, plastic bags encourage moisture loss and soften the crust. The worst place for storing bread is the fridge: bread gets stale most quickly in temperatures just above freezing.

29

Use natural yeasts to make a sourdough starter by mashing 3 or 4 skinned potatoes in their cooking water. Mix 220g (8oz) of this with the same of flour and 2 tablespoons of sugar. Leave, loosely covered in a warmish place for up to a week. The natural yeasts will soon get to work. Store in the fridge.

30

Sourdough bread has a delicious acidic tang.

Take the starter out of the fridge at least 12 hours before use. Mix 220g (8oz) of the sourdough starter with 570g (1½lb) of flour, proceeding as for ordinary bread. Feed the remaining starter lovingly with more flour and water and it should never fail you.

31

Rolls come in all shapes and sizes.

Use the standard bread dough. You'll get about a dozen rolls for every 450g (1lb) pound of flour used, but don't worry about making them exactly equal in size. Shape by rolling into a ball, or by rolling out into a long strip and tying it in a knot. Dust with flour and bake for 15 minutes.

32

For a quick loaf

(or if you're out of yeast),

use baking powder. In the bowl, mix 450g (1lb) of white flour and I teaspoon each of salt and bicarbonate of soda. Stir in about 300ml ($^1/_2$ pint) of buttermilk and a little sunflower oil. Knead for one minute, shape into a round loaf, slash the top and bake for 35 minutes.

33

Bread-and-butter pudding

is a core part of the British yeoman diet. Line a dish with 4 slices of buttered stale white bread minus crusts. Cover thickly with mixed dried fruit, then a layer of creamy custard (dashed with rum). Add other layers of bread, fruit and custard and top off with bread. Stand for 1 hour then bake another hour.

34

Pizza is even simpler to make than bread. For one pizza, mix 275g ($^1/_2$lb) white flour with a pinch of salt. Stir in about 50ml (2fl oz) water and yeast mix (but no oil or fat). Knead, leave for an hour, then pull or roll flat and thin. Spread on a drained tin of tomatoes (plus oregano), sprinkle over grated Mozzarella and bake for 15 minutes in a hot oven.

35

Buy yourself

a ceramic or stone slab for baking pizzas

and other breads. You can also use an unglazed earthenware floor tile for this. A slab gives an infinitely superior crust and a more consistent texture. Remember to pop it in the oven when you turn it on so it heats slowly from cold. Otherwise it will crack!

36

Add something exotic to your bread. After the first rising, try adding chopped stoned olives, or sunflower seeds, or herbs, or chopped sundried tomatoes (though not all together of course). Experiment with combinations of ingredients – sage and onion, for example, or walnut and apricot.

37

Summer pudding is the best dessert ever.

Simmer 1kg (2lb) of mixed summer fruits in sugared water and drain. Line a basin with slices of white bread (stale and de-crusted) soaked in the juice. Put in the fruit and cap with more soaked bread. Refrigerate overnight with a weighted plate on top. Turn out onto a plate.

38

Rye flour adds a dark pungency to bread.

Mix 1 part of rye to 2 parts wheat flour, and include 300ml ($^1/_2$ pint) of warm milk. This encourages the rye (which is low in gluten) to rise. Proceed as for ordinary bread, though try adding caraway seeds at the final rising.

39

Pompe a l'huile

(oil pump) is a strange sort of name, but it's still

a treat in south-west France. Roll out 450g (1lb) of white dough and dot with butter. Roll up and refrigerate for 2 hours. Roll out again to 12mm ($^1/_2$ inch) thick and let rise. Bake for 15 minutes, then drizzle with walnut oil and sugar. Wash down with a glass of Marcillac.

40

Here's **another use for a stale white loaf – bread sauce.**

In a saucepan, heat up 450ml (3/4 pint) milk, 110g (4oz) breadcrumbs, a big lump of butter, 12 cloves, a chopped onion. Simmer gently for 10 minutes, then leave to cool. Season and remove cloves (if you can) before serving.

41

Steam is a vital ingredient in some crusty breads, notably French-style baguettes. Just before you slide the dough into the oven, fine-spray the loaves with cold water. Repeat at 5- or 10-minute intervals. The bread comes out beautifully crisp and crunchy.

42

Revive

(reasonably) stale

bread by popping it in the oven.

Ten minutes at 160°C should be sufficient. Heat doesn't merely crisp up the loaf; it makes the remaining water move about inside and soften the starch molecules.

43

There are plenty of **good uses for stale bread.** It's tougher than fresh, and will keep its spongey texture even when wet. Use slices in puddings (see Tips 32 and 34), chunks in salads, or breadcrumbs in stuffings and coatings for fried food. Or fry cubes with olive oil and garlic to use as croûtons in soups.

44

Always make sure your

new-baked bread has cooled completely before storing.

This can take three or four hours. Any residual heat will cause a build up of moisture in store, which in turn encourages mould.

45

Getting

big air pockets in your loaves?

There are **several possible causes:**

you may be using too much yeast; you may not be kneading as long or as thoroughly as necessary; or you may be leaving the dough to rise for too long in the tins.

46

Christmas bread should be fragrant and exciting but not too sweet.

So melt 25g (1oz) butter and beat in 300ml ($^1/_2$ pint) of Guinness and 50ml ($^1/_4$ pint) of syrup. Add this to the standard dough mixture, along with cardamom seeds and grated orange zest. After baking, glaze the top with honey.

47

Be aware of **added chemicals – they can affect your dough's performance.**

Bad rising may be due to excess chlorine in the water (use filtered instead), extra iodine in salt (use sea salt), or bleaching and 'improving' agents in the flour. If in doubt, use the purest ingredients you can source.

48

Impanata,

or bread pie, is

a Sicilian version of the Cornish pasty.

Oil a pan and line with 6mm ($^1/_4$ inch) dough. Fill with either chopped Swiss chard, tomato and oil, or spinach, Parmesan and Ricotta. Top off with more thin dough, prick a few holes in it and bake for 30 minutes.

49

Be very gentle with your dough once it has risen. A jolt or thump can cause it to deflate like a burst cycle tyre. Take especial care when transferring tins of dough to the oven – it's easy to knock or even drop one. The result: heavy bread.

50

Beat the smoke alarm – with bread. If you're roasting meat, put two or three thick slices of white bread in the pan. They will absorb a lot of the fat so it can't smoke. Thus you can stop the alarm going off and lessen that charcoal smell in the kitchen.

Andrew Langley

Andrew Langley is a knowledgeable food and drink writer. Among his formative influences he lists a season picking grapes in Bordeaux, several years of raising sheep and chickens in Wiltshire and two decades drinking his grandmother's tea. He has written books on a number of Scottish and Irish whisky distilleries and is the editor of the highly regarded anthology of the writings of the legendary Victorian chef Alexis Soyer.

THE LITTLE BOOK OF
BARBECUE
TIPS
ANDREW LANGLEY

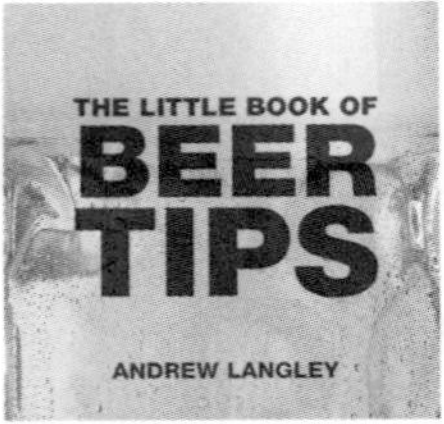
THE LITTLE BOOK OF
BEER
TIPS
ANDREW LANGLEY

THE LITTLE BOOK OF
HERB
TIPS
WILLIAM FORTT

THE LITTLE BOOK OF
POKER
TIPS

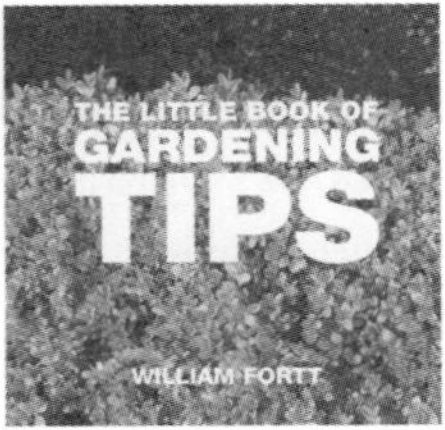
THE LITTLE BOOK OF
GARDENING
TIPS
WILLIAM FORTT

THE LITTLE BOOK OF
CHEFS'
TIPS
RICHARD MAGGS

THE LITTLE BOOK OF
SPICE
TIPS
ANDREW LANGLEY

THE LITTLE BOOK OF
GOLF
TIPS
PETER FRENCH

THE LITTLE BOOK OF
TIPS
SERIES

THE LITTLE BOOK OF
CHEESE
TIPS
ANDREW LANGLEY

THE LITTLE BOOK OF
WINE
TIPS
ANDREW LANGLEY

THE LITTLE BOOK OF
AGA
TIPS 2
RICHARD MAGGS

THE LITTLE BOOK OF
COFFEE
TIPS
ANDREW LANGLEY
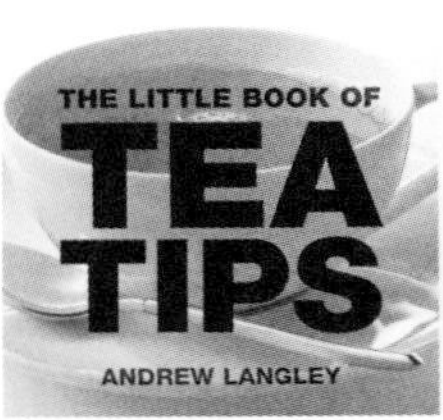
THE LITTLE BOOK OF
TEA
TIPS
ANDREW LANGLEY

THE LITTLE BOOK OF
AGA
TIPS 3
RICHARD MAGGS

THE LITTLE BOOK OF
AGA
TIPS
RICHARD MAGGS

THE LITTLE BOOK OF
CHRISTMAS
AGA
TIPS
RICHARD MAGGS

THE LITTLE BOOK OF
RAYBURN
TIPS
RICHARD MAGGS

THE LITTLE BOOK OF
BRIDGE
TIPS
CHRIS JONES

THE LITTLE BOOK OF
CHESS
TIPS
PETER FRENCH

THE LITTLE BOOK OF
FISHING
TIPS
MICK DEVENISH

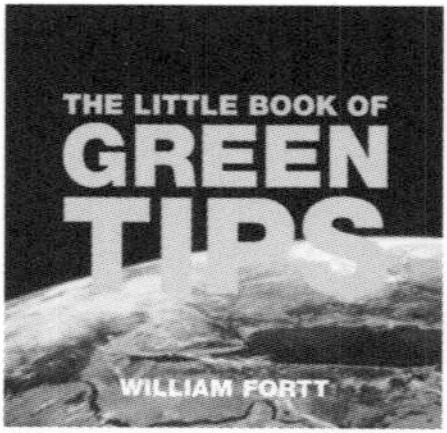
THE LITTLE BOOK OF
GREEN
TIPS
WILLIAM FORTT

THE LITTLE BOOK OF
KITTEN
TIPS
ANDREW LANGLEY

MARMITE
THE LITTLE BOOK OF
MARMITE
TIPS

THE LITTLE BOOK OF
PUPPY
TIPS
ANDREW LANGLEY

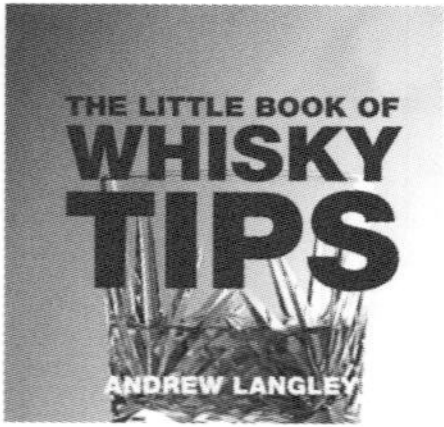
THE LITTLE BOOK OF
WHISKY
TIPS
ANDREW LANGLEY

THE LITTLE BOOK OF
TRAVEL
TIPS
MEGAN DEVENISH

Little Books of Tips from Absolute Press

Aga Tips
Aga Tips 2
Aga Tips 3
Backgammon Tips
Barbecue Tips
Beer Tips
Bread Tips
Bridge Tips
Cake Decorating Tips
Cheese Tips
Chefs' Tips
Chess Tips
Christmas Aga Tips
Coffee Tips
Fishing Tips
Gardening Tips
Golf Tips
Green Tips
Hair Tips
Herb Tips
Houseplant Tips
Kitten Tips
Marmite Tips
Nail Tips
Olive Oil Tips
Poker Tips
Puppy Tips
Rayburn Tips
Scrabble Tips
Spice Tips
Tea Tips
Travel Tips
Vinegar Tips
Whisky Tips
Wine Tips

All titles: £2.99 / 112 pages